604

FISH

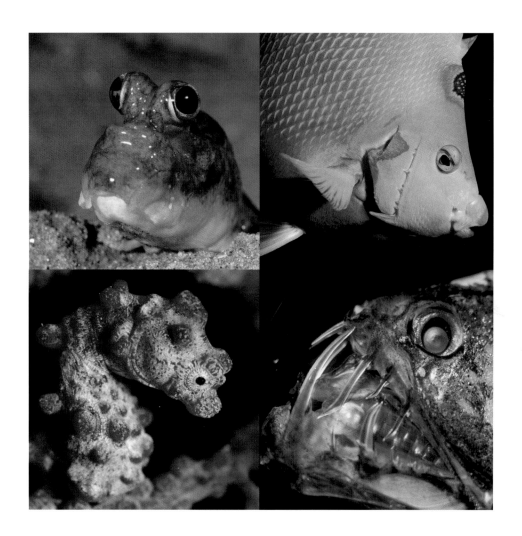

Sarah Wilkes

WORLD ALMANAC® LIBRARY

Please visit our web site at: www.worldalmanaclibrary.com
For a free color catalog describing World Almanac® Library's list of high-quality books
and multimedia programs, call 1-800-848-2928 (USA) or 1-800-387-3178 (Canada).
World Almanac® Library's fax: (414) 332-3567.

Library of Congress Cataloging-in-Publication Data

Wilkes, Sarah, 1964-
    Fish / by Sarah Wilkes.
       p. cm. — (World Almanac Library of the animal kingdom)
     Includes bibliographical references and index.
     ISBN 0-8368-6210-4 (lib. bdg.)
     1. Fishes—Juvenile literature. I. Title.
    QL617.2.W55 2006
    597—dc22   2005051693

This North American edition first published in 2006 by
World Almanac® Library
A Member of the WRC Media Family of Companies
330 West Olive Street, Suite 100
Milwaukee, WI 53212 USA

This U.S. edition copyright © 2006 by World Almanac® Library. Original edition
copyright © 2006 by Hodder Wayland. First published in 2006 by Hodder Wayland, an
imprint of Hodder Children's Books, a division of Hodder Headline Limited, 338 Euston
Road, London NW1 3BH, U.K.

Subject Consultant: Jane Mainwaring, Natural History Museum
Editor: Polly Goodman
Designer: Tim Mayer
Illustrator: Jackie Harland
Picture research: Morgan Interactive Ltd and Victoria Coombs
World Almanac® Library art direction: Tammy West
World Almanac® Library editor: Carol Ryback
World Almanac® Library cover design: Jenni Gaylord

Photo credits: (t) top; b (bottom); l (left); right (r).
Cover photograph: an Indo-Pacific blue tang.
Title page (clockwise from top left): a mudskipper, an angelfish, a viperfish, and a sea horse.
Chapter borders (top to bottom): macro images of the scales of a broomtail wrasse, a coral
grouper, an emperor angelfish, a sabre squirrelfish, and a blue triggerfish.
CORBIS: / Jeffrey L. Rotman cover. Ecoscene: / Adrian Davies 4; / Reinhard Dirscheri 5,
29, 34, 37, 41; / Phillip Colla 11, 12, 13, 14; / Jeff Collett 25, 35, 36; / Clive Druett 26;
/ Michael Gore 27; / John Liddiard 39, 43; / Chinch Gryniewicz 42. naturepl.com:
/ Brandon Cole 6; / Reijo Juurinen/Naturbild 7, 28; / Florian Graner 8; / Bruce Rasner 10;
Doug Perrine 9, 20; / Georgette Douwma 15; / Jeff Rotman 17, 23; / Juan Manuel Borrero
18; / Doc White 19, 21, 33; / Chris Gomersall 22; / Herman Brehm 24; / Jeff Foott 30, 31;
/ Julian Partridge 32; / Fabio Liverani 38; / Aflo 40.

Printed in China

1 2 3 4 5 6 7 8 9 10 09 08 07 06

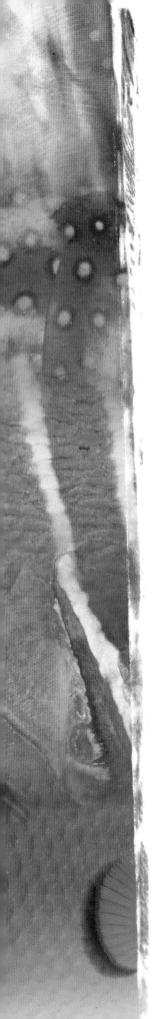

CONTENTS

It is not possible to include information about every fish species in this book. A taxonomic chart for fish appears on page 44.

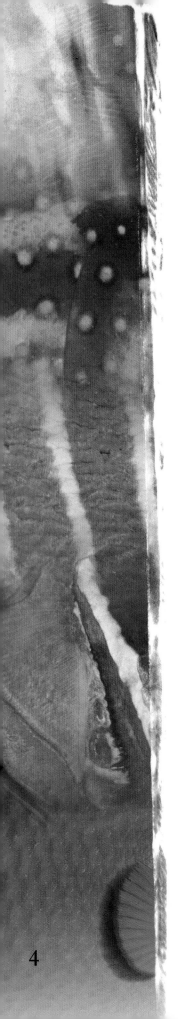

WHAT ARE FISH?

Fish swim the waters of the world, no matter how cold, warm, deep, or shallow. Altogether, about 27,500 species of fish, some of which look nothing like normal fish, exist. Their sizes range from whale sharks that can measure up to about 39 feet (12 meters) to the male stout infantfish measuring a mere 0.28 inches (0.7 centimeters) in length.

Fish features

Fish belong to a large group of animals called vertebrates. All vertebrates have a vertebral column—a series of small bones that runs down their back. Fish bodies have smooth lines to facilitate swimming. Their overall body shapes are adapted to their particular aquatic habitat. Reef fish tend to have bodies flattened at the sides to enter narrow spaces. Some bottom-dwellers are flat top-to-bottom, and pelagic (ocean roaming) fish have long bodies. Most fish have paired fins (pectoral and pelvic), single median fins (dorsal, caudal, and anal), and a muscular tail that ends in a vertical caudal fin. Scales cover the skin of most fish species. The lateral line, a special sense organ made of pressure-sensitive receptors, runs down both sides of their body. Fish breathe underwater through gills. As water flows through the gills, oxygen passes from the water into the blood.

Typical Bony Fish

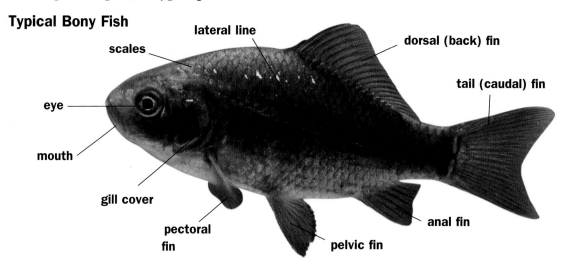

A typical bony fish, such as this goldfish (*Carassius auratus*), has two sets of paired fins (pectoral and pelvic) and a number of single fins.

CLASSIFICATION

Biologists have identified about two million unique organisms. They examine the similarities and differences between organisms and group together those with shared characteristics. The classification system moves through general to specific categories until each organism receives an exact binomial classification: a "last" name—the genus—and a "first"name—the species. The animal kingdom is divided into phyla (singular: phylum). Each phylum is divided into classes (also super- and subclasses), which are divided into orders (also super- and suborders) and then into families, genera (singular: genus), and species. A genus and species names a single organism—such as a blue shark—that differs from all other organisms. In most cases, only members of the same species can reproduce with each other to produce fertile offspring.

The classification of the blue shark (*Prionace glauca*) appears in this chart.

KINGDOM: Animalia
|
PHYLUM: Chordata
|
CLASS: Chondrichthyes
|
SUBCLASS: Elasmobranchii
|
ORDER: Carcharhiniformes
|
FAMILY: Carcharhinidae (requiem sharks)
|
GENUS: *Prionace*
|
SPECIES: *glauca* (blue shark)

Use the first letter of each word in this sentence to remember the classification order:
Kings **P**lay **C**hess **O**n **F**ridays, **G**enerally **S**peaking.

Reproduction
Most fish lay eggs that hatch into tiny fish called fry. Some fish carry their eggs within their body instead and give birth to live young.

Classes
Fish are classified into one of four classes: two for jawless fish (Myxini and Cephalaspidomorphi); the cartilaginous fish (Chondrichthyes); and the bony fish (Osteichthyes). This book dicusses the four classes and the orders within them. It also examines the features of the divisions and how they differ from one another. It is not possible to cover all the orders of fish in this book. A taxonomial tree of the classification system appears on page 44.

A lizardfish is a type of bony fish. It is a predator. The one below holds a smaller fish in its mouth.

Jawless Fish (Myxini and Cephalaspidomorphi)

Jawless fish are bizarre-looking fish that do not resemble other fish. Their ancestors first appeared more than five hundred million years ago. They consist of two classes: hagfish (Myxini) and lampreys (Cephalaspidomorphi). Only a few species of each type of jawless fish still exist.

Hagfish are long, slender, and pinkish in color. They grow to about 28 inches (70 cm) and are best known for the large quantities of sticky slime they produce.

Shared features

Jawless fish have a round mouth with a sucker and a rasping tongue instead of a jaw. They have long bodies and look somewhat like eels. They have small, unpaired fins. Instead of scales covering their skin, jawless fish (especially the hagfish) produce large quantities of protective slime. They have no visible gill covers on the outside of their body. Instead, their gills open through tiny pores (tiny holes) in the body wall.

Lampreys

Lampreys have a sucker with a fringed edge surrounding their mouth. Rather than a pair of nostrils, they have a single nasal opening, either at the end of their snout or on top of their head. Their flexible spine is made of cartilage, which helps lampreys swim more powerfully. Their brain case also is made of cartilage.

Life cycle of the lamprey

Some lampreys live in freshwater while others, such as the sea lamprey, live in saltwater. Both must breed in freshwater, so sea lampreys return to freshwater to lay their eggs. Lamprey eggs are large and surrounded by a tough egg case. The eggs hatch into larval fish known as ammocete larvae, which bury themselves in freshwater mud. Lamprey larvae look very different from the adult form. They undergo metamorphosis to change into adults. Young sea lampreys return to saltwater to mature.

Lamprey food

Adult lampreys are parasites. A parasite is an organism that lives on another organism, or host, and harms the host in the process. Lampreys use their sucker and teeth to attach themselves to the skin of other fish and suck their blood. In some environments, such as the Great Lakes, lampreys present a serious pest because they harm the native fish populations. Lampreys are "exotic" species (not native) to the Great Lakes. They were introduced from other parts of the world via the ballast tanks of ships, which were emptied and rinsed in the Great Lakes.

Hagfish

The wormlike hagfish lives on the seabed, where it scavenges the dead bodies of animals. It uses rows of horny teeth on its tongue to rasp at food. A ring of tentacles surrounds its mouth. The hagfish eats by pushing its head inside the bodies of rotting animals and sucking the flesh into its mouth.

Adult lampreys attach themselves to fish and marine (saltwater) mammals using a sucker with pointed teeth. Once attached, the lamprey creates a wound on its prey's skin using its rasping tongue and sharp teeth. It feeds on the prey's blood and body tissue. Lampreys grow to about 32 inches (80 cm) in length.

KEY CHARACTERISTICS
MYXINI AND CEPHALASPIDOMORPHI

- **Mouth and sucker instead of jaws.**
- **Single nasal opening.**
- **Tiny pores instead of a gill cover.**
- **Saliva contains a chemical that prevents the blood of the host from clotting.**

CARTILAGINOUS FISH (CHONDRICHTHYES)

The great white shark is among the most feared of all animals. This large fish is one of many hundreds of different species of shark, which are grouped together with rays, skates, ratfish, and chimeras in a class called cartilaginous fishes (Chondrichthyes).

The ratfish (*Chimaera monstrosa*) lives at depths of 100–200 feet (30–60 m), but it has been found as deep as 3,300 feet (1,000 m). Its first dorsal fin is triangular with a spine in front, while its second dorsal fin is long and continuous.

Cartilaginous skeleton

Cartilaginous fish have a skeleton made of cartilage instead of bone. This is the same flexible material that shapes our ears and nose. The jaws and teeth of sharks are made of calicified cartilage—not true bone.

Other features distinguish cartilaginous fish from other classes of fish. Unlike bony fish, which have a swim bladder filled with air to provide buoyancy, cartilaginous fish do not have a swim bladder. Their oily liver provides some buoyancy, but cartilaginous fish must keep swimming to keep from sinking.

The rough skin of cartilaginous fish is covered in tiny, teethlike structures called dermal denticles. Cartilaginous fish have a series of gill slits rather than one single gill cover. They have either five, six, or seven slits on each side of their head, through which water is expelled after passing over the gills.

Spiracle

All cartilaginous fish have an opening behind each eye called a spiracle. The spiracles in sharks provide oxygenated blood directly to the eye and brain through a separate blood vessel. The spiracles are fairly small or even absent in a number of sharks, particularly the fast-swimming sharks. In rays and skates, the spiracle is much larger and actively pumps water over the gills, allowing these fish to breathe while buried in the sand (*see page 15*).

(*see page 15*)

KEY CHARACTERISTICS
CHONDRICHTHYES

- **Skeleton made of cartilage.**
- **Body covered in dermal denticles.**
- **Gill slits rather than gill covers.**
- **Spiracle behind each eye.**
- **Internal fertilization.**
- **No swim bladder.**
- **Asymmetrical tail fin.**

Reproduction

Unlike other fish, fertilization in cartilaginous fish is internal. The male fish inserts a pair of organs called claspers into the female to fertilize her eggs. The female then produces a few large eggs. A large yolk nourishes each egg, so that by the time the young fish hatch, they are well developed. Since cartilaginous fish produce only a few eggs (between 2 and 300) compared with the thousands produced by bony fish, female sharks are very careful about where they place the eggs. For example, the female Port Jackson shark screws her eggs into rock crevices. The eggs may take up to fifteen months to develop. The young sharks are miniature versions of their parents.

Rays and some sharks, such as the lemon shark, do not lay eggs. The females retain the eggs inside their body and give birth to live young, called pups. Species that give birth to live young are called viviparous.

Subclasses

Cartilaginous fish are divided into two subclasses: Holocephali and Elasmobranchii. Holocephali is made up of ratfish and chimeras. Elasmobranchii is much larger and contains the sharks and rays. It is divided into thirteen orders.

The lemon shark (*Negaprion brevirostris*) gives birth to live young in shallow nursery grounds between April and September. The pups remain in the nursery grounds for several years before swimming out into the open ocean. This pup is being born tail first.

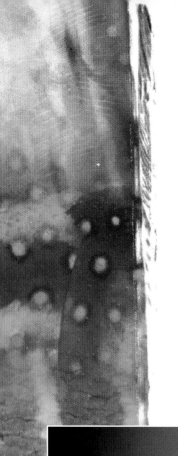

SHARKS, RAYS, AND SKATES (ELASMOBRANCHII)

In 1976, a team of researchers made an exciting discovery: a gigantic shark that weighed slightly more than 1,600 pounds (725 kilograms) and measured 15 feet (4.5 m) long. It was like no other shark, with a broad head and an extra-wide mouth. Biologists named it "megamouth" (*Megachasma pelagios*).

Only thirty sightings of the megamouth shark (*Megachasma pelagios*) have been confirmed in the Indian, Pacific, and Atlantic Oceans.

Sharks, rays, and skates belong to the subclass Elasmobranchii. This large group of cartilaginous fish is divided into a number of superorders, including the frilled, cow, dogfish, angel, and saw sharks (Squalomorpha); the bullhead, carpet, ground, and mackerel sharks (Galeomorpha); and rays and skates (Batoids).

Shark features

There are approximately 360 species of sharks. Most species are about 8 feet (2.5 m) long, but they range in size from the 10-inch (25-cm) green dogfish to the giant whale sharks, which may grow up to 66 feet (20 m) long. Unlike bony fish, sharks do not have a swim bladder, so they must swim constantly to keep from sinking. They have a streamlined, tapering body with a strong, muscular tail that powers their swimming. Their tail fin splits into a distinctive, asymmetric caudal fin with a larger upper than lower lobe. Sharks have large, triangular-shaped pectoral fins, held out at right angles to their bodies, which they use for steering and balance. When they swim just under the surface, their dorsal fin sticks out of the water. Sharks also have an eyelid known as the nictitating membrane that protects each eye.

Internal gills

Sharks have internal gills that take up oxygen from the water. The water enters the mouth, flows over the gills, and out through the gill slits. The number of gill slits on the side of the head is a distinguishing feature. Most sharks have five gills, but some sharks, including the cow sharks, have six gills. The seven-gill shark is the only species to have seven gill slits.

Shark teeth

Just like their scales, sharks' teeth are triangular. They grow in rows along the jaws. Sharks regularly lose their teeth when feeding. Their replacement teeth simply move into place to fill the empty spots—much like a conveyor belt loaded with replacement teeth.

The great white shark's Latin name, *Carcharodon carcharias*, means "ragged tooth." The largest great white sharks grow to about 23 feet (7 m) in length— that's about the same as two small cars parked end to end. Great whites average 13 to 16 feet (4 to 5 m) long.

KEY CHARACTERISTICS
ELASMOBRANCHII

- **Five or more gill slits.**
- **Spiracle behind each eye.**

The whale shark (*Rhincodon typus*) reaches lengths of up to 66 feet (20 m). It feeds on plankton by opening and closing its mouth so that water flows through its gill chambers. Dermal denticles that line the gills and the pharynx help trap the plankton.

Food

Sharks are highly effective predators, with superbly developed senses that help them find their prey. Ironically, the largest shark of all, the whale shark, is a harmless plankton feeder.

Senses

In addition to their lateral lines, sharks have a unique sensor system in their snout called the Ampullae of Lorenzini. These sensors detect electrical signals generated by the muscle movements of prey, including those of fish lying under the sand. Sharks also have excellent sight and smell. Their sense of smell is many thousands of times better than that of a human, enabling them to detect one drop of blood in 25 gallons (95 liters) of water.

Prey

Sharks feed on a range of prey animals, including fish, marine mammals, and birds. They also scavenge dead bodies. Sharks that feed near the surface, such as mako and thresher sharks, are streamlined, powerful swimmers. The mako shark, a type of mackerel shark, swims at speeds of up to 60 miles (97 kilometers) per hour in short bursts to catch fast-moving tuna and marlin. The heat generated by muscles in their body and tail warms their blood and helps them function well in cold water.

sluggish. Shellfish eaters, such as porbeagle sharks, have coarse, crushing teeth.

Plankton feeders

Whale, basking, and megamouth sharks feed on plankton. They each have a large, wide mouth and can take in large quantities of water into their gill chambers. The water is filtered by the gills as it passes out through the gill slits. The plankton is then swallowed. Whale and basking sharks swim across oceans in search of food. The megamouth lives deep in the ocean and swims up to the surface at night to feed on plankton.

Life cycle

Depending on the species, sharks take from three to sixteen years to reach sexual maturity. In viviparous sharks, the gestation period—the time for embryos to develop into baby sharks—ranges from six months to two years. Viviparous sharks average twelve pups in a litter, but there may be as few as one or two.

STRONG SWIMMERS

- The mako shark holds the speed record for long-distance travel. It can swim 1,324 miles (2,130 kilometers) in thirty-seven days, an average of about 36 miles (58 km) per day.

- The bull shark also is known as the river whaler because it swims up some of the world's largest rivers, such as the Amazon in South America. It has been found more than 1,900 miles (3,000 km) from the ocean.

The horn shark (*Heterodontus francisci*) is a bottom-dwelling shark that grows to about 4 feet (1.2 m). It has rounded fins, a blunt snout, ridges over the eyes, and a spine that sticks out of the dorsal fin. This one is feeding on squid eggs on the seabed.

Rays and skates

Rays and skates differ greatly in appearance from sharks. There are 456 species of rays and skates, divided into five orders: skates (Rajiformes); guitarfish (Rhinobatiformes); electric rays (Torpediniformes); stingrays and eagle rays (Myliobatiformes); and sawfish (Pristiformes).

Flattened bodies

The main feature of rays and skates is a body that is flattened from top to bottom. The width of their body ranges from just 10 inches (25 cm) to 7 feet (2.1 m). The pectoral fins of rays and skates are greatly enlarged to look like a pair of wings held out to the sides of their body. As they swim, these fins gently rise up and down—like a flapping bird. Their tails are long and slender. In some species, the tail bears sharp, poisonous barbs that can inflict painful wounds. Some rays can produce a severe electric shock to stun prey.

Biologists use the distinctive markings on the underside of mobula and manta rays to identify and track individuals. Mobula rays (*Mobula* sp.) are smaller than manta rays and tend to travel in shoals. There are nine species of mobula rays.

Habitat and food

Skates and many rays live on the seabed, where they feed on prey such as crustaceans and worms. Their body is adapted to bottom living. For example, their mouth is located on their lower surface. Their teeth are hard, flattened plates ideal for crushing the shells of invertebrates including crabs and clams. Another adaptation is the position of their spiracle, which is located on the dorsal (in this case, upper) surface. If the spiracle were positioned on the ventral (in this case, lower) surface, they would get a mouthful of muddy water.

Many rays live in groups in estuaries and other places with sandy seabeds. They also roam the open ocean and kelp beds of coastal waters. Rays feed by moving through masses of plankton or shoals of small fish, turning slowly from side to side. They use large, flaplike lobes on either side of their head to fan prey into their broad mouth.

The blue spotted stingray (*Taeniura lymna*) uses two plates in its mouth to crush the shells of crabs, prawns, and mollusks. Its tail is slightly longer than its body, and it has a spine (the stinger) about halfway down its tail.

WHAT'S THE DIFFERENCE?

RAYS
- **Long, whiplike tails without fins.**
- **Give birth to live young.**

SKATES
- **Thick tail with dorsal fins.**
- **Lay eggs.**

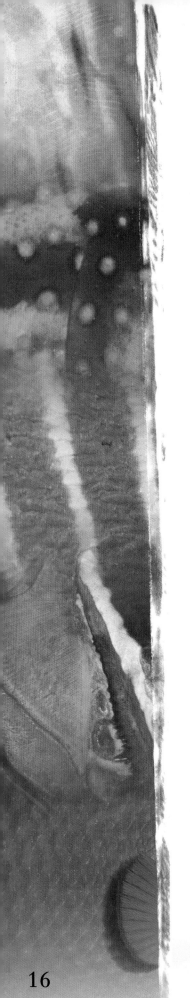

BONY FISH (OSTEICHTHYES)

There are more than 24,000 species of bony fish, making Osteichthyes the largest of the four classes of fish. Bony fish are found in every aquatic habitat, and a few species, such as the walking catfish and the mudskipper, can even crawl on land. Bony fish are a major source of protein for millions of people.

Bony fish features

The main characteristic of bony fish is the presence of a bony skeleton. They have a swim bladder to help their buoyancy and a single gill cover, called an operculum, on each side instead of gill slits. The opercula allow a current of water to pass out from the gills during exhalation while preventing water from entering during inhalation.

Life cycle

Most bony fish lay eggs that hatch within days into tiny fish. Some fish, however, including common aquarium fish such as guppies, swordtails, and mollies, carry their eggs inside their bodies and give birth to live young. Most bony fish do not provide any care for their offspring, but there are a

Breathing With Gills

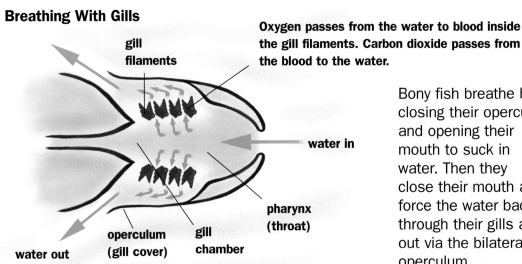

gill filaments

Oxygen passes from the water to blood inside the gill filaments. Carbon dioxide passes from the blood to the water.

water in

pharynx (throat)

operculum (gill cover)

gill chamber

water out

Bony fish breathe by closing their opercula and opening their mouth to suck in water. Then they close their mouth and force the water back through their gills and out via the bilateral operculum.

few exceptions. For example, some female African cichlids carry their eggs and then their young in their mouth. The young fish swim out of the mouth and feed close to the female; at the first sign of danger, they return to her mouth.

Subclasses

The class of Osteichthyes is divided into two subclasses: Actinopterygii and Sarcopterygii. Actinopterygii are ray-finned fish. Their fins are made from webs of skin supported by bony spines. Unlike sharks, which have a very limited range of pectoral movement, bony fish can move easily and rotate their paired fins while turning or to act as brakes. Two groups within Actinopterygii are the primitive ray-finned fish known as Chondrostei, which include the paddlefish and gar, and the more advanced ray-finned fish, known as Teleostei.

Sarcopterygii

The subclass Sarcopterygii contains primitive fish with fleshy fins. A lobe of bone and muscle extends into their fins. This subclass includes lungfish and the ancient coelacanth. Their fleshy fins are flexible and in the lungfish support the body of the fish while it is on land. There are six species of lungfish and a single species of coelacanth. The lungfish is unusual because it has gills and a single lung formed from its swim bladder. A good blood supply to the lungs enables this fish to survive out of water for long periods of time. The first specimen of a living coelacanth known to science was caught in a net off the coast of South Africa in 1938. It was nicknamed "old four legs" because its pectoral and pelvic fins resembled limbs. Before that, scientists believed coelocanths had been extinct for millions of years.

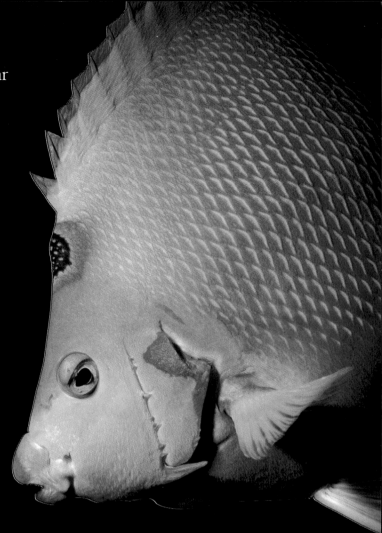

The beautifully colored queen angelfish (*Holacanthus ciliaris*) has a tall, narrow body. It feeds on a variety of marine invertebrates, especially sponges, jellyfish, and corals, as well as on plankton and algae.

KEY CHARACTERISTICS
OSTEICHTHYES

- Bony skeleton.
- Gill covers (opercula).
- Swim bladder.

PRIMITIVE RAY-FINNED FISH (CHONDROSTEI)

Primitive ray-finned fish are among the most unusual-looking fish within the subclass Actinopterygii. This superorder, native only to the Northern Hemisphere, consists of four orders: bichirs (Polypteriformes); sturgeon and paddlefish (Acipenseriformes); gars (Semionotiformes); and bowfins (Amiiformes).

Gars have needlelike teeth and a heavily scaled body. The largest gars grow up to 12 feet (3.7 m) long.

Chondrostei features

Members of Chondrostei are large fish with a skeleton made of part bone and part cartilage. The skull and some of the fin supports consist of bone, while the body and tail are supported by a cartilaginous backbone. Some species have a sharklike asymmetrical tail fin. Most of these fish lack scales on their body. When present, however, the scales usually are diamond shaped and heavy looking. One of the distinctive features of Chondrostei fish is that their backbone turns sharply upward into the upper lobe of the tail fin. Some species also have a rostrum, which is an extension from the head past the mouth. The rostrum is particularly well developed in the paddlefish.

All primitive ray-finned fish have gills for obtaining oxygen. The gar, the bowfin, and some of the bichirs also have a swim bladder lined with blood vessels that work somelike a lung. These fish can gulp air if the oxygen level of the water falls and they cannot obtain enough oxygen through their gills.

Habitat

Most of these fish live in freshwater. For example, the bichir lives in the Nile River as well as in some West African rivers. The predatory gars are native to North America. Their elongated body and long jaws make gars resemble the pike. Gars hang motionless in vegetation waiting for prey animals to pass close by before darting out. Their median fins are positioned far back near their tail fin. This fin arrangement is similar to the feathers on an arrow and helps gars move fast through the water.

Paddlefish live in large rivers such as the Mississippi, where there is plenty of plankton in the water. They open their mouth and filter the water as it flows through their gills. Paddlefish feed at night. During the day, they rest at the bottom of deep rivers. There are a few saltwater paddlefish species as well, such as the European sturgeon. This fish spends its adult life in the ocean. It migrates hundreds of miles (kilometers) to lay its eggs in freshwater rivers.

KEY CHARACTERISTICS
CHONDROSTEI

- Skeleton is part bone and part cartilage.
- Backbone ends in the upper lobe of the tail (caudal) fin.
- Most species lack scales or have diamond-shaped scales.

EELS (ELOPOMORPHA)

Eels and the lesser-known halosaurs, tarpons, and tapirfish make up the superorder Elopomorpha. These fish look quite different from one another, but they have one thing in common—they all start life the same way: as nearly transparent, ribbonlike larvae.

The superorder Elopomorpha is made up of five orders: halosaurs (Albuliformes); eels (Anguilliformes); tarpons (Elopiformes); spiny eels and tapirfish (Notacanthiformes); and swallowers (Saccopharyngiformes).

A humpback cleaner shrimp searches the mouth of a yellow-edged moray eel (*Gymnothorax flavimarginatus*) for tasty tidbits. These eels hide in crevices in a coral reef and wait for prey to pass by.

Elopomorpha features

Eels have a long, snakelike body. More than one hundred vertebrae in their backbone make their body incredibly flexible. Their small dorsal and anal fins extend along the length of their body. Most eels lack scales. Eels generally have a good sense of smell but relatively poor eyesight.

Halosaurs live at extreme depths, even to 11,000 feet (3,350 m), in frigid water at the very bottom of the oceans. They have an elongated body about 22 inches (55 cm) long, and a well-developed lateral line that is highly sensitive to vibrations that occur in their lightless habitat. Tarpon, meanwhile, live along the American coasts of the Atlantic Ocean and the western coast of Africa. Female tarpon can live about fifty years, while male tarpon live about thirty years. Tarpon reproduce when about six years old.

Predators

Most Elopomorpha are predators. Tarpon larvae absorb nutrients through their skin. As their body shape changes to become more fishlike, they gradually become herbivorous and carnivorous, until as fully mature adults, they become completely carnivorous. Halosaurs feed on marine worms, crustaceans, and bottom-living invertebrates. Moray eels hide in rock crevices and seize passing prey. Many moray eels also have teeth strong enought to crush shells.

Life cycle

All the fish in Elopomorpha have a similar, complicated life cycle. Adult European eels live in freshwater rivers. To breed, they swim downstream and across the North Atlantic Ocean to an area known as the Sargasso Sea (between Bermuda and the Azores). The journey takes seven months, during which time the eels do not eat. They mate, lay their eggs, and die in the Sargasso Sea. The eggs hatch into ribbonlike, translucent larvae that look nothing like the adult. The larvae drift in currents that carry them east across the Atlantic Ocean, a journey that takes two-and-a-half years. Then they undergo metamorphosis and change into cylindrical "glass eels" known as elvers, with fins, scales, and pigmentation. The young complete their journey by swimming up rivers to grow into adults.

The bizarre-looking gulper eel can reach lengths of 6 feet (2 m). It is found at depths of 6,200 feet (1,900 m). Its huge mouth can swallow prey much larger than itself, and its stomach stretches to accommodate large meals.

HERRING (CLUPEOMORPHA)

The Atlantic herring (*Clupea harengus*) has a distinctive forked tail fin. All the fins are soft and lack spines. The silvery scales scatter light and help camouflage the fish.

Herring, pilchards, and anchovies are small fish that live in large groups called shoals. Theses species form an important link in marine food chains. Herring and their relatives belong to the superorder Clupeomorpha, which is made up of a single order, called Clupeiformes.

Herring features

All of the roughly 360 species in this order have a similar appearance. Many are silver. Their streamlined body shape allows them to slip through the water with ease. Their bodies are covered in large scales, and the fins are well developed. Herring, pilchards, and anchovies are known to have good hearing. Their swim bladder is linked to their ears, which increases their sensitivity to sound.

Life cycle

Large shoals of Atlantic herring return to the same spawning grounds each year. Each female lays up to forty thousand tiny eggs that are fertilized by the males. The eggs sink to the seabed, where they hatch into minute larvae

KEY CHARACTERISTICS
CLUPEOMORPHA

- Body covered by large scales.
- Swim bladder linked to the ears to improve hearing.
- Live in shoals.
- Filter feeders.

that look somewhat like tiny eels. The larvae migrate to the upper layers of the ocean and become part of the plankton. Plankton constists of millions of tiny plants (phytoplankton) and animals (zooplankton).

Food chains

Herring, pilchards, and anchovies are filter feeders that eat plankton. They open their large mouths and sieve food from the water. Zooplankton spend the daylight hours in deep water and migrate to the surface to feed in the safety of darkness. Herring and their relatives have learned to follow this movement of their food, so each day they migrate from the depths to the surface, too.

Threats

Herring, pilchards, and anchovies live in large shoals and attract the attention of many predatory fish such as salmon, tuna, and marlin. Seals, dolphins, and seabirds also eat shoal fish. Anchovies and herring are important commercial fish and are caught by trawlers around the world. Unfortunately, shoal fish have been overfished and their numbers are falling. This depletion affects the other animals in the food chain as well.

SHOALS

A shoal is made up of many fish but it moves as one individual. In a shoal, each fish swims parallel to its neighbor using sight, hearing, and its lateral line to keep in position. A shoal often twists and turns as one unit. Only bony fish display this particular shoaling behavior. It's safer for fish to swim in shoals than alone. Predators find it difficult to pick out a single fish in a shoal because they are distracted by so many fish moving together.

Small, silvery fish with blue-green backs, anchovy (*Engraulis* sp.) never grow larger than 8 inches (20 cm).

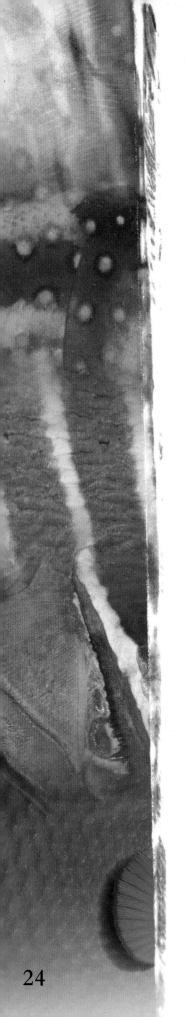

Catfish (Ostariophysi)

Catfish and their relatives live mostly in freshwater lakes, rivers, and streams. They belong to the superorder Ostariophysi, which includes about six thousand species divided into five orders: milkfish; minnows and carp; characins, tigerfish, tetras, and piranhas; electric eels and knifefish; and catfish.

Ostariophysi features

Despite their varied physical appearances, the fish in this superorder share an internal feature called the Weberian apparatus. This unusual arrangement of bones in the vertebral column transmits sounds from the swim bladder to the inner ear. It gives these fish excellent hearing. Milkfish have a slightly different bone

ELECTRIC EEL

Despite its name, the electric eel is not an eel but a type of knifefish. This large, nearly 9-foot (2.75-m) fish has a long anal fin and a tail that tapers to a point. It has three "electric" organs called the Sachs, main, and hunter organs. The Sachs' organ helps it navigate by producing weak pulses of electricity. The main and hunter electric organs produce stronger bolts of electricity up to 650 volts, powerful enough to kill prey—or even a human after repeated jolts.

The electric eel (*Electrophorus electricus*) lives in the Amazon River basin in South America. It prefers to live in marshy or stagnant water.

arrangement. Instead of a Weberian apparatus, they have modified ribs that transmit sounds from the swim bladder to the ear. Many fish in Ostariophysi communicate using sound.

The body of the striped catfish (*Plotosus lineatus*) tapers toward its tail. It can reach lengths of about 14 inches (35 cm). Juvenile striped catfish often form shoals.

Catfish

Catfish have a flattened head and barbels. A barbel is somewhat like a whisker. Taste buds on the barbels help the fish find food. Catfish often live in murky water and have poor eyesight. Most species have smooth, scaleless skin, although a few species, such as the bushy mouth catfish, are exceptions. The enlarged scales of the bushy mouth catfish look like plates of armor. The majority of catfish have sharp pectoral and dorsal spines. In some species, these spines can release poisons. Many catfish also release an alarm substance when injured, which sends a signal to others in the vicinity to flee.

> **KEY CHARACTERISTICS**
> OSTARIOPHYSI
> - **Most species have the Weberian apparatus for hearing.**
> - **Catfish have taste buds on their barbels and most have scaleless skin.**

Carp

Carp are deep-bodied, freshwater fish. They have been introduced to rivers, ponds, and lakes around the world as a source of food. The highly flexible mouth of the carp allows it to rummage through the mud and bottom sediment of ponds and lakes when searching for food. The teeth in these fish are not located in the jaws. Instead, carp grind their food using teeth in the back of their throat.

Catfish, such as this channel catfish (*Ictalurus punctatus*) native to North America, use their barbels to find food in murky water.

Feeding

Many members of the catfish superorder, such as tetras, hatchet fish, and zebrafish, are favorites for home aquariums because they are colorful and easy to keep. Their natural habitat is tropical rivers, where they move around in shoals for safety and feed on plankton and plants. These species are in turn eaten by larger predatory fish as well as birds. These fish perform an important role in the food chain of rivers.

Catfish live on the ocean and river floors. They are nocturnal fish (active at night) and feed alone, relying on their sense of touch and hearing to navigate. The wels is the largest of the catfish. It has two extra-long barbels on its upper jaw and four smaller ones on its lower jaw. Like all catfish, it uses taste buds on its barbels to find food in the gloom. It is a predator that feeds on crustaceans, small fish, ducks, small geese, and even otters.

Tigerfish are large predators that form shoals in African rivers. They grow up to 6 feet (1.8 m) long. These fish catch and swallow their prey whole, head first. They attack prey up to half their own length.

Piranhas

Most varieties of piranhas are harmless, eating water plants, fruits, and seeds. The red-bellied piranhas, however, are aggressive predators. Their small, sharp, triangular teeth are spaced so that when the jaw closes, the teeth interlink, and they can slice off pieces of their prey. The lower jaw sticks out in front of the upper jaw and gives the fish a strong bite.

Piranhas feed at dawn and at dusk. They wait, hidden in the shadows, until they detect prey, then dart out to catch it. Most of their prey are small fish and insects, but piranhas also attack larger animals, such as sloths, capybaras, and deer, that fall in the water from trees or while crossing rivers.

Piranhas have triangular teeth with razor-sharp edges. Their large, powerful lower jaw sticks out beyond the upper jaw so that the teeth fit together like a trap. The piranha rips its prey into small pieces.

SALMON (PROTACANTHOPTERYGII)

Salmon and their relatives are large, powerful predatory fish found around the world. Salmon, trout, char, pike, and grayling belong to the superorder Protacanthopterygii. It contains three orders: salmon and trout; argentines and smelts; and pikes.

The brown trout (*Salmo trutta fario*) lives in rivers, where it feeds on insects, crayfish, mollusks, frogs, and rodents. It spawns between late autumn and early winter in shallow rivers with a gravel bed. The female digs a nest in the gravel and lays about two thousand eggs.

Salmon features

The fish in this superorder are characterized by their long bodies; powerful, muscular tails; and large tail fins. Their streamlined bodies have few, if any, scales, and their small fins do not stick out much or restrict movement. The pelvic fins are positioned well back on the body, and there is a small, fleshy fin called the adipose fin located on the upper edge near the tail. The arrangement of fins on these fish is ideally suited to the way they feed: They tend to ambush their prey, shooting forward with a burst of speed.

Predators

Salmon and their relatives are mostly predatory. They have a long jaw and sharp teeth for catching prey. A pike's teeth are particularly large; pike are renowned for swallowing prey almost half their own size. The hatchet fish is a deep-sea fish with a very tall body. It feeds mostly by sucking invertebrates into its wide mouth. There is little food in the ocean depths, so these fish must be able to swallow any prey they find—however large.

Spook fish

Spook fish (*Dolichopteryx binocularis*) are bizarre-looking deep-sea fish. Their pectoral fins are greatly extended to half the length of their body. This fish gets its name from its strange, tubular-shaped eyes, which resemble a pair of binoculars that enable it to see above the water's surface. Spook fish have a second pair of eyes, located on the side of the tubular eyes, for side vision.

Life cycle

Some members of the salmon superorder, such as the pike and grayling, live in freshwater for their entire life. Others, such as the capelin, live in saltwater. Capelin live in shoals and spend most of the year in the Arctic Ocean. They migrate to coastal waters, where they spawn on beaches. Capelin lay their eggs at high tide so the eggs get buried in the sand. This protects the eggs. During the next high tide, the young fish hatch and swim out to sea. A few species, such as the salmon, trout, and eulachon, have a life cycle that involves both freshwater and saltwater (*see page 30*).

The pike (*Esox luciu*) is a predatory fish that lives in freshwater. It lurks among the weeds, waiting for prey to pass. Pikes eat mainly fish, but they also catch water voles and ducklings. They grow to lengths of 60 inches (150 cm) and weigh up to 55 pounds (25 kg).

Salmon life cycle

Some salmon make one of the most amazing journeys of the animal world. These large, active fish travel from freshwater to the ocean and then back to freshwater to complete their life cycle. All species of salmon undergo a similar journey. The one featured on this page is the journey of the sockeye salmon, which breeds in rivers along the Pacific coast of North America and lives its adult life in the northern Pacific Ocean. The sockeye salmon also is called the red or blue back salmon.

The eyes of the salmon embryos are just visible inside these eggs. Only a few eggs survive to adulthood.

Below: The male sockeye salmon (*Oncorhynchus nerka*), on left, has a hooked jaw and a humped back, while the female (on right) has a more rounded body.

Migration

The life cycle of the sockeye salmon starts when the breeding adults return to the rivers in which they were born. They swim up the rivers to the breeding grounds, often overcoming natural obstacles such as rapids, waterfalls, and fallen trees, and jumping up special "salmon ladders" alongside dams. Scientists are uncertain how salmon navigate back to their spawning grounds. It may involve their highly developed sense of smell or an ability to navigate by the stars. When ready to breed, the adult salmon change their appearance. Both sexes develop a green head, and the sides of their bodies turn bright red. The male develops a humpback and a hooked jaw.

Alevins (newly hatched salmon) have an enormous yolk sac that provides all the nutrition they need for the first weeks of their lives. Alevins remain in the redd (nest) until their yolk sac is absorbed and they become free-swimming fry (young fish). Alevins need cold, clear, oxygen-rich water to remain healthy. Aquatic insects and other fish prey on the alevins.

Spawning occurs in shallow waters, where there is gravel on the riverbed. The female uses her tail to dig out a nest, called a redd, in the gravel. She lays up to forty-five hundred eggs that are fertilized by the male. After spawning, the adult salmon die.

Young fish

The eggs hatch after about sixty days. The tiny fish, called alevins, grow rapidly. They stay in the gravel for about four months before starting their journey downstream. Sockeye salmon breed only in rivers that drain into a lake. The young fish can spend a year growing, reaching about 4 inches (10 cm) in length. After one year, the older fish, called fingerlings, complete their journey by swimming to the ocean. Their bodies undergo changes in order to live in saltwater. They spend three to four years in the North Pacific Ocean feeding and maturing. At about four years of age, they are ready to breed.

SPAWNING

Sockeye and chinook salmon swim as far as 1,000 miles (1,600 km) upstream to spawn, while chum, coho, and pink salmon spawn closer to the ocean. Kokanee salmon live their entire lives in freshwater lakes. Some kokanee spawn in streams that feed into the lake, while others spawn in the shallow water along the shore. Like the sockeye salmon, both the kokanee and Pacific salmon die after spawning; Atlantic salmon do not.

JELLYNOSE FISH AND DRAGONFISH (STERNOPTERYGII)

Jellynose fish and dragonfish live in the abyss. This inhospitable habitat is pitch dark, exceedingly cold, and under extreme water pressure. Jellynose and dragonfish are specially adapted to survive in this environment.

Sternopterygii features

The superorder Sternopterygii consists of two orders: jellynose fish (Ateleopodiformes) and dragonfish and viperfish (Stomiiformes). These deep-sea fish have a strange appearance. Jellynose fish have an elongated, flabby body. They live on the seabed. Dragonfish and viperfish also have an elongated body with an extra-large head and jaws that can open remarkably wide. Their teeth are like needles. These scaleless fish have dark bodies with a velvety skin. Many species produce an eerie light using special body organs.

The viperfish is one of the fiercest predators of the deep. It has a large mouth and sharp, fanglike teeth. The teeth are so long that they do not fit inside its mouth. Researchers believe the viperfish impales prey on its teeth by swimming at prey at high speeds.

Surviving the deep

One of the main problems of living in the ocean depths is the lack of food. No light penetrates the abyss, so no plants can grow. Few animals live there, and those that do feed on any food they find. Sharp teeth help them grip prey. Deep-sea denizens (inhabitants) usually have large, flexible jaws to swallow prey whole. As their stomach fills up from a meal, it pushes backward on their heart and gills.

Some deep-sea fish have special ways of luring their prey. They make their own light using light-producing organs called photophores. Dragonfish, for example, have photophores along their sides and around their mouth. They also have a sort of fleshy "fishing pole" that extends over their mouth with a photophore at the end. They wave this dangling lure around to attract prey.

Extra order: Lizardfish (Cyclosquamata)

Cyclosquamata is a superorder of relatively small fish up to about 20 inches (50 cm) long. Named after their lizardlike appearance, lizardfish sit on the seabed, propped up by their stiff pectoral fins. Most live at relatively shallow depths, although a few species have been found several thousand feet (meters) down. Their mottled body blends well with their surroundings, especially on coral reefs.

The cartilaginous skeleton of the jellynose fish helps compensate for extreme water pressure in the abyss. Its large head has a bulbous nose, and their long body tapers toward the tail. Jellynose fish range in size, with the longest reaching up to 7 feet (2.1 m).

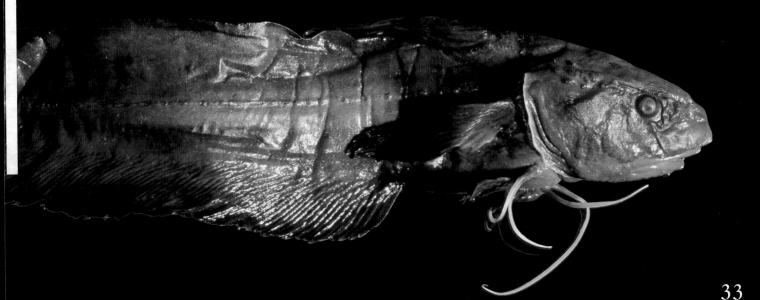

COD AND ANGLERFISH (PARACANTHOPTERYGII)

The single barbel on the chin of this Atlantic cod (*Gadus morhua*) is clearly visible. Cod grow up to 51 inches (130 cm) long and weigh as much as 77 pounds (35 kg).

Paracanthopterygii is a diverse superorder of fish. It includes cod—one of the most economically important fish in the world—along with other commercially fished species such as hake, haddock, and whiting. The commercial fish form large shoals. This superorder also includes a group of benthic (bottom-living) fish called anglerfish and frogfish. Many of the fish that belong to Paracanthopterygii are found on the seabed.

Paracanthopterygii features

Most members of Paracanthopterygii have a long and relatively narrow body. One distinctive feature is the arrangement of the fins. The dorsal fin is divided into three sections, while the pelvic and anal fins are positioned well forward. The mouth usually is found on the ventral surface, where it is ideally positioned for bottom feeding. Many species in this superorder have a single barbel covered in taste buds on their chin.

Food chains

Cod is an important part of the marine food chain. Huge shoals of cod swim just above the seabed, feeding on smaller fish such as capelin and herring. Seals, dolphins, and predatory fish, such as marlin, prey on cod.

Cod life cycle

Adult cod form large shoals that follow regular migration routes between their breeding grounds and feeding grounds. This makes the cod shoals ideal fish for harvesting. Cod breed in spring. A single female cod can lay at least one million eggs, which are fertilized by the males. She lays such a large number of eggs because the survival rates are very low; only a small number of eggs hatch and grow to adulthood. The large number of eggs attracts many predators.

Frogfish and anglerfish

These strange-looking relatives of cod have a patterned body that is camouflaged on the seabed. The irregular body shape of the frogfish makes it difficult to see when it is still. Anglerfish are named after their dangling lure—a modified part of their dorsal fin that hangs in front of their mouth to attract prey.

KEY CHARACTERISTICS
PARACANTHOPTERYGII

- Most have a long and relatively narrow body.
- Dorsal fin is divided into three sections.
- Pelvic and anal fins are positioned well forward on the body.
- Ventrally positioned mouth.
- Many have a single barbel on their chin.

The frogfish (*Antennarius* sp.) has a thick skin covered in scales called dermal spicules that resemble the warts of a toad. Frogfish live in sponges in shallow waters around coral reefs. They use their pectoral and pelvic fins to "walk" slowly across the reefs.

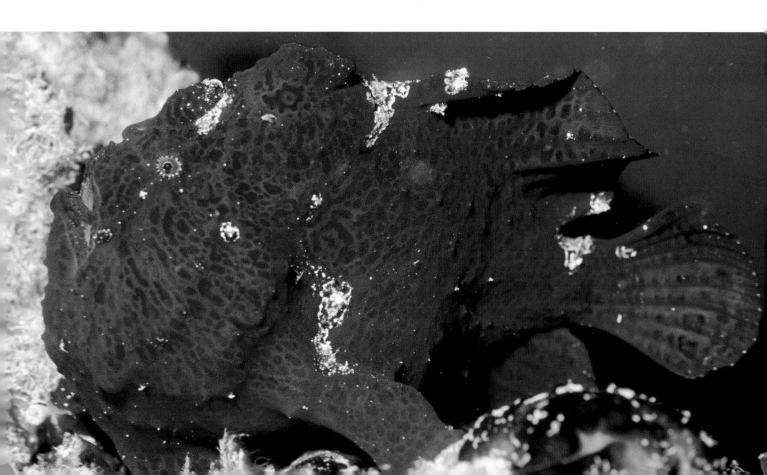

SPINY-RAYED FISH (ACANTHOPTERYGII)

This ragged-fin lionfish (*Pterois antennata*) has a striped body and delicate, fan-shaped fins. The fins are tipped with poisonous spines.

More than half of all fish species belong to the superorder Acanthopterygii, the spiny-rayed fish. This varied group contains thirteen orders of fish including the sea horse, grouper, perch, angelfish, anemone fish, and plaice.

Spiny-rayed features

Spiny-rayed fish are characterized by the presence of stiff, bony spines that form the front edge of the dorsal and anal fins. In some fish, such as lionfish, these spines are armed with poison. Their paired pelvic fins are positioned far forward along the body so that the pectoral and pelvic fins appear joined. The scales of these fish have tiny spines that give the surface a rough texture. In some species, the scales are enlarged to form bony plates, while others have long spines. A few species have lost their scales altogether. Spiny-rayed fish have a mouth that can be extended to ingest prey.

Body shapes

The body shapes of the fish within this superorder vary greatly. Flatfish look as if they are lying on one side. Both eyes end up on the upper surface. For the first six weeks or so, the larvae of flatfish look much like that of other fish larvae. As they begin changing, their body becomes flatter. One eye moves across the head so that both eyes lie close together. The upper side of the body becomes darker and speckled, providing camouflage when the fish lies on the seabed. Flatfish swim parallel to the ocean bottom.

The sea horse is another oddly shaped, tiny fish. Its head, with its long snout, resembles a horse's head, and spiny scales cover its body. A long, prehensile tail allows it to anchor to the reef or plants. The ocean sunfish, on the other hand, is one of the world's heaviest fish. It looks almost circular when viewed from the side. Sunfish hold out their triangular dorsal and anal fins like blades.

KEY CHARACTERISTICS
ACANTHOPTERYGII

- Stiff, bony spines form the front edge of the dorsal and anal fins.
- Pelvic fins positioned well forward.
- Most have scales with tiny spines.

Sea horses are covered in armorlike scales. They swim upright, propelled by tiny fins. This pygmy sea horse (*Hippocampus bargibanti*) is perfectly camouflaged against the coral on which it lives. It is tiny—just 0.8 inches (2 cm) long.

Habitat

Most spiny-rayed fish are marine (saltwater) animals that live in coastal waters, on coral reefs, and in the open ocean. A few, such as mudskippers, live on muddy beaches and can move from pool to pool across the sand.

The mudskipper (*Periophthalmus* sp.) has a large head with bulging eyes. It can flip across the sand from one rock pool to another, breathing through its skin when out of the water. There are several species of mudskippers, the largest reaching 10 inches (25 cm) in length.

Food chains

Spiny-rayed fish play an important role in marine food chains. Their larvae form part of the plankton that is eaten by large invertebrates, other fish, and some whales. Grunions, for example, feed on the plankton and are themselves preyed upon by larger fish.

The fast-swimming predators of this superorder include tuna, marlin, swordfish, and barracuda. Tuna have a long, streamlined body, sickle-shaped pectoral fins, and a crescent-shaped tail. They can lower their dorsal fin into a groove to improve streamlining and increase speed. Muscle heat generated as tuna swim helps keep them warm and active in cold water. Tuna swim thousands of miles (km) across the open oceans in search of shoals of anchovies, herring, and other fish.

Flying fish live near the surface and feed on plankton. They have an unusual way of escaping from predators such as tuna and marlin. They swim at speeds of up to 37 mph (60 kph) and can propel themselves into the air. Their paired fins are stiff and enlarged so they can glide over the water for up to 700 feet (200 m).

Camouflage

Many spiny-rayed fish are camouflaged to avoid their predators. The sea dragon has leafy flaps attached to its fins to break up its outline and allow it to hide among seaweed. Stonefish are slow-moving predators found near the seabed. They have a colored, scaleless body that blends in with the color of a rocky seabed. Stonefish have thirteen dorsal spines loaded with poison to protect themselves from predators.

The wolffish (*Anarhichas lupus*) is a solitary fish that hides in rock crevices. It feeds by grabbing passing animals, such as crabs, sea urchins, and starfish. Its jaws are exceptionally strong and are equipped with massive teeth to crush the body of its prey.

SIAMESE FIGHTING FISH

The male Siamese fighting fish (*Betta splendens*) is fiercely territorial and will fight another male to death in order to defend its territory or win a female. If another male approaches, the fish opens its large, colorful fins to give the impression of being bigger. Its colors also intensify.

When a male is ready to mate, he builds a bubble nest for the eggs by carrying air in his mouth, coating it with saliva, and spitting it out in bubbles, which stick together on the water's surface.

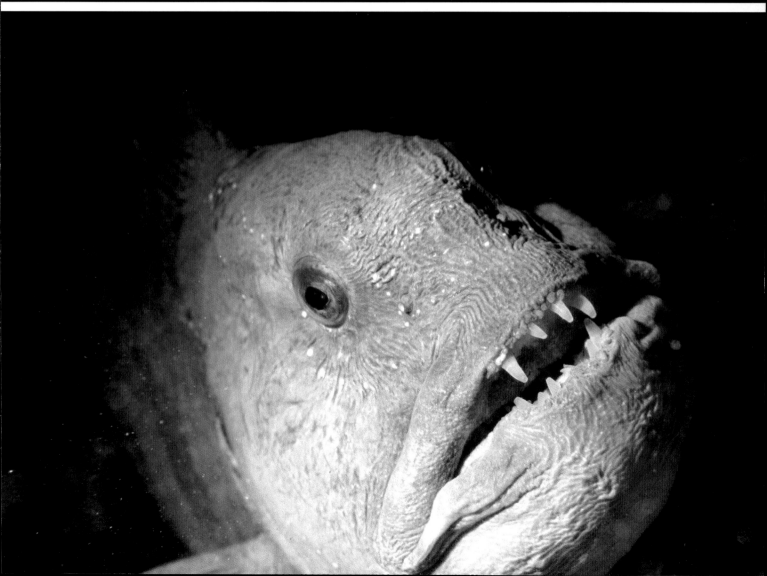

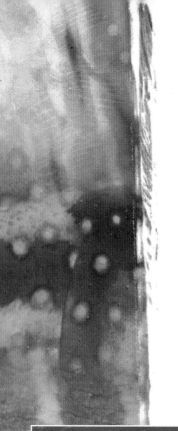

ON A CORAL REEF

Coral reefs are one of the most diverse habitats in the world. Many species of plants, invertebrates, and fish live on coral reefs.

Tiny animals called corals that are related to sea anemones build coral reefs. Living corals secrete a limestone skeleton around themselves. When they die, the skeleton is left behind. Coral reefs develop in warm, coastal waters in tropical regions of the world. The corals need clear and unpolluted water to survive. The world's largest coral reef is the Great Barrier Reef, off the coast of Australia. The second-largest reef is the long barrier reef which lies off the coast of Belize in Central America.

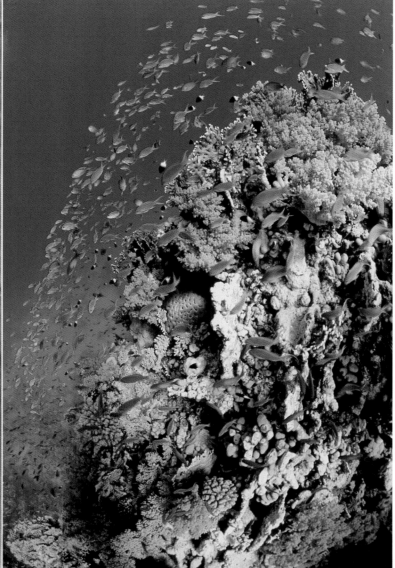

Fish habitat

Coral reefs are home to many fish, from large sharks to tiny gobies. Reefs make excellent fish habitats because of their plentiful food supply. For example, parrot fish feed on the corals, while sharks hunt near coral reefs for prey. Coral reefs also provide protection from predators. Shoals of small fish, such as glass fish, anthias, and bigeyes, swim among the coral. The large numbers of invertebrates and shoals of small fish attract predators that patrol the reef looking for prey. Solitary fish, such as moray eels, lurk in crevices, while groupers swim close to the reefs and stay in the same area for many years.

Fish are among the most common animals on a coral reef. Shoals of brightly colored fish swim around the coral while moray eels lurk in crevices. The small fish attract predators such as sharks.

The pink anemonefish (*Amphiprion perideraion*) lives among sea anemones, which are marine animals that resemble flowers. Few predators venture near a sea anemone's stinging tentacles. Anemonefish, however, can live in a sea anemone. Some anemonefish have natural protection against a sea anemone's stings, but other anemonefish simply endure the stings in order to live in a sea anemone. Anemonefish have the capability to change from male to female when necessary.

Some fish have a mutualistic relationship with the coral animals. In this type of relationship, both animals benefit from the association. For example, the clown anemonefish lives among the poisonous tentacles of the sea anemone. The fish is immune to the poison thanks to a layer of mucus over its scales. The sea anemone provides the clown anemonefish with shelter and safety from predators. In return, the sea anemone feeds on scraps of food left by the fish.

Mangrove swamps

Mangrove swamps, found along tropical coasts and often near coral reefs, are another important fish habitat. Many reef fish come to mangrove swamps to breed. The young fish grow up in the nutrient-rich environment of the swamps before swimming out to the reef as adults. Mangroves are also important to the survival of the reef itself because the roots of the mangrove trees trap silt carried in rivers and stop it from being carried out to the ocean and covering the corals.

REEF FACTS

- Coral reefs provide a home for more than a quarter of all marine life, yet they take up less than 1 percent of the ocean floor.

- Coral reefs attract thousands of visitors and bring a lot of money into an area. The value of coral reef tourism is twenty-seven times that of the world's marine fisheries—a very good reason for conserving them!

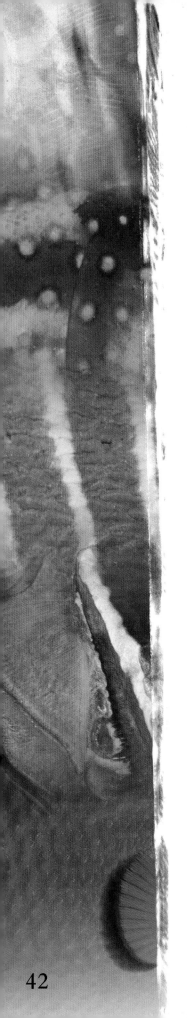

UNDER THREAT

Fish, like many other types of animals, are affected by water pollution, loss of habitat, and global warming. Overfishing is also a major problem around the world.

Pollution

People traditionally used rivers, lakes, and oceans as dumping grounds for trash, sewage, and chemical and radioactive wastes, all of which pollute the water. Fish are sensitive to any pollutants that reduce the oxygen content of the water and to poisons that can harm or kill them.

Coral reefs

Coral reefs respond poorly to pollutants. Changes in water quality can easily damage coral reefs. They also are sensitive to water temperatures—even the slightest change not only kills corals but also leads to fish deaths. Scuba diving is an increasingly popular activity. Divers help boost the economies of impovished areas by spending money on hotels, in restaurants, and on other tourist attractions.

A spill of detergent off the coast has produced a mass of foam that is smothering this rocky shore. Chemical spills kill many of the invertebrate animals living in shallow coastal waters.

Thousands of divers visit coral reefs around the world daily. Touching corals or kicking them with a swim fin causes much harm. Most scuba divers respect the underwater environment they are visiting and take great care when diving.

Overfishing

Overfishing is a global problem. Enormous "factory" fishing ships equipped with refrigerated holds and freezers harvest huge amounts of fish in one trip. Nature cannot compete with the efficiency of this international fishing industry. For example, the fishing pressure on Atlantic cod has depleted the stocks so much that yearly harvests have dropped remarkably in the last two decades. Sharks also are severely overfished. Sharks take a long time to mature and do not produce many eggs or young, making them especially susceptible to overfishing. Shark "finning" is one of the most objectionable practices regarding shark fishing. Sometimes, sharks are caught just so their fins can be chopped off for shark-fin soup. While the animal is still alive, the rest of the body is then dumped back into the sea to drown. While some countries have banned finning, it is still a popular shark fishing method.

Scuba divers sometimes damage the more accessible coral reefs. When divers touch the living parts of reefs, they wipe away the mucus that protects the tiny corals from disease and water contaminants.

Pets

Some fish species are bred for home aquariums, but far too many reef fish are caught in the wild by squirting cyanide into the water, which causes liver damage to the fish and kills the reefs.

Conservation

What can be done? Some governments protect coral reefs, mangroves, and other fish breeding grounds. Laws that control overfishing often limit catches according to species. Regulations on the sizes and types of fishing nets used allow young fish, dolphins, sea turtles, shark, rays, and other "bycatch" to escape. Careful steps taken now will lead to a healthy marine environment in the future.

SHARK FINNING

Shark catches are increasing because of the demand for their fins in shark-fin soup and in various natural medicines. Shark finning is a cruel practice in which a shark is caught, its fins cut off, and while still alive, dumped back into the sea. Unable to swim, the shark sinks to the ocean floor, where it eventually dies. Many nations ban shark fishing and impose fines and jail terms for anybody caught finning sharks. Sadly, some Asian nations consider shark-fin soup a delicacy and continue this repulsive practice.

FISH CLASSIFICATION

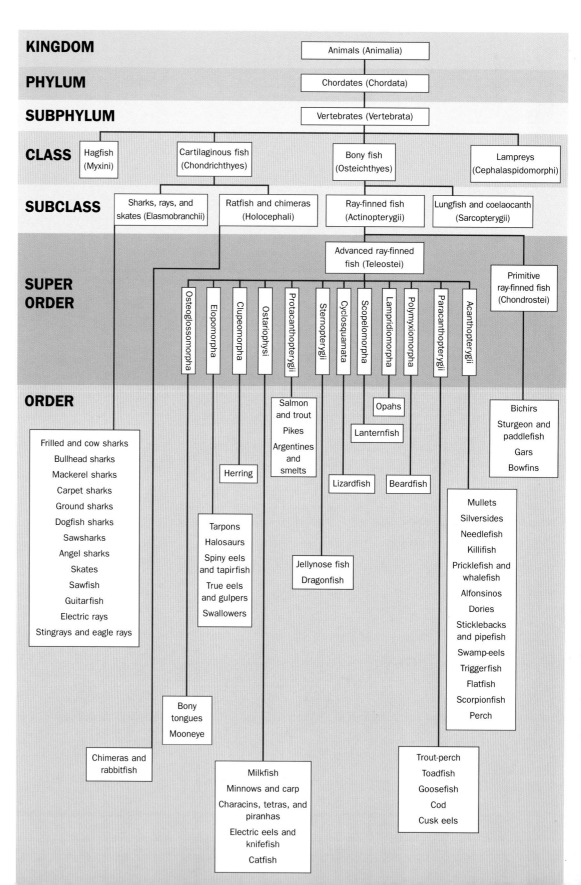

KINGDOM	Animals (Animalia)
PHYLUM	Chordates (Chordata)
SUBPHYLUM	Vertebrates (Vertebrata)

CLASS: Hagfish (Myxini) · Cartilaginous fish (Chondrichthyes) · Bony fish (Osteichthyes) · Lampreys (Cephalaspidomorphi)

SUBCLASS: Sharks, rays, and skates (Elasmobranchii) · Ratfish and chimeras (Holocephali) · Ray-finned fish (Actinopterygii) · Lungfish and coelaocanth (Sarcopterygii)

SUPER ORDER: Advanced ray-finned fish (Teleostei) · Osteoglossomorpha · Elopomorpha · Clupeomorpha · Ostariophysi · Protacanthopterygii · Sternopterygii · Cyclosquamata · Scopelomorpha · Lampridiomorpha · Polymyxiomorpha · Paracanthopterygii · Acanthopterygii · Primitive ray-finned fish (Chondrostei)

ORDER:

- Frilled and cow sharks
- Bullhead sharks
- Mackerel sharks
- Carpet sharks
- Ground sharks
- Dogfish sharks
- Sawsharks
- Angel sharks
- Skates
- Sawfish
- Guitarfish
- Electric rays
- Stingrays and eagle rays

- Chimeras and rabbitfish

- Bony tongues
- Mooneye

- Tarpons
- Halosaurs
- Spiny eels and tapirfish
- True eels and gulpers
- Swallowers

- Herring

- Milkfish
- Minnows and carp
- Characins, tetras, and piranhas
- Electric eels and knifefish
- Catfish

- Salmon and trout
- Pikes
- Argentines and smelts

- Jellynose fish
- Dragonfish

- Lizardfish

- Opahs
- Lanternfish

- Beardfish

- Mullets
- Silversides
- Needlefish
- Killifish
- Pricklefish and whalefish
- Alfonsinos
- Dories
- Sticklebacks and pipefish
- Swamp-eels
- Triggerfish
- Flatfish
- Scorpionfish
- Perch

- Trout-perch
- Toadfish
- Goosefish
- Cod
- Cusk eels

- Bichirs
- Sturgeon and paddlefish
- Gars
- Bowfins

44

GLOSSARY

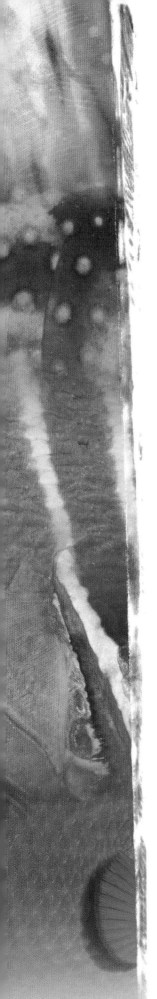

abyss the ocean depths.

adapted changed to best cope with the environment.

anal fin a single fin near the anus.

aquatic relating to water.

ballast tanks shipboard holding tanks that contain adjustable levels of water or air that provide stability according to seagoing conditions.

barbel a whiskerlike structure on the snout of a fish; often has taste buds.

benthic bottom-dwelling.

buoyancy the ability to remain afloat in a liquid.

camouflage colors and patterns that blend in with the background.

cartilage flexible connective tissue that forms the skeleton of rays and sharks.

cartilaginous fish fish with a skeleton made mostly of cartilage.

crustaceans animals with an exoskeleton and jointed limbs; for example, crabs and lobsters.

dermal denticles tiny, toothlike projections of skin.

dorsal related to the back.

dorsal fin the single fin on the back.

endangered animals or plants at risk of becoming extinct.

estuary the place where a river enters the ocean.

extinct permanently gone.

fertilization the joining of an egg and sperm to produce a new living thing.

fin a thin flap of skin, supported by spines, used by aquatic creatures to swim, balance, and steer.

fish stocks the number of fish in a particular area.

fry newly hatched fish.

gestation period the developmental time between mating and giving birth.

gill covers flaps that cover and protect the gills.

gills underwater breathing organs.

host an organism upon which another organism lives or feeds.

invertebrate an animal that lacks a backbone, such as a snail or insect.

kelp bed masses of giant seaweed known as kelp, found in fairly shallow coastal waters, that form a habitat for a number of aquatic species.

larva a young animal that undergoes metamorphosis to become an adult.

lateral line a strip of sensors that runs from behind the head and down the sides of the body of aquatic creatures.

lobe a rounded part of a fin.

marine related to saltwater.

median fins the dorsal (back), anal, and caudal (tail) fins.

metamorphosis a change in body shape during an animal's life cycle.

migrate to move to a new habitat in a different location, usually for breeding or feeding.

nictitating membrane a protective third eyelid found on some animals.

nocturnal active at night.

order in the classification system, a category of organisms that is more general than a family but more specific than a class.

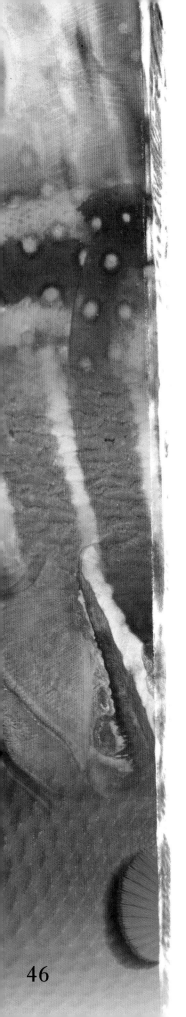

GLOSSARY (CONTINUED)

parasites organisms that harm the host upon which they live or feed.

pectoral fins paired fins located near the rib area of the skeleton.

pelagic ocean-roaming.

pelvic fins paired fins located near the hip area of the skeleton.

pharynx the throat.

photophore a light-producing organ.

phytoplankton tiny plants that float at the mercy of water currents.

plankton tiny plants and animals that float in the upper layers of the ocean, moving at the mercy of the currents.

predator an animal that catches and kills other animals, usually for food.

prehensile able to grab or wrap around an object.

prey animals vulnerable to attack by predators.

primitive an early, unrefined stage of development.

rasping a rough, irritating surface.

receptor something that responds to an external stimulus, such as light.

rostrum a body part that extends from the head to beyond the mouth.

scavenge to feed on dead and decaying bodies.

scuba diving swimming underwater while breathing through a cylinder of compressed air that is carried along at all depths.

sensory receptors structures that recognize environmental changes, such as light, heat, or taste.

shoal a group of fish.

skeleton the rigid internal framework, made of bone or cartilage, of an animal.

spiracle a hole behind the eyes of cartilaginous fish.

streamlined shaped with smooth surfaces that facilitate movement.

subclass in the classification system, organisms with characteristics that fall into special divisions more particular to the class designation than to the order designation.

superorder in the classification system, organisms with intermediate characteristics that fall into special divisions but differ from the true "order" classification.

tentacles long, usually sensitive extensions from the bodies of some animals that may contain stinging cells for catching prey.

translucent semi-transparent.

tropical places near the equator that experience hot and humid weather most of the year.

ventral surface the lower or belly surface on the body of an animal.

vertebrate an animal with a vertebral column (backbone).

viviparous animals that give birth to live young.

yolk the portion of an egg, consisting of protein and fat, from which an embryo gets its nourishment.

zooplankton tiny animals that float at the mercy of water currents.

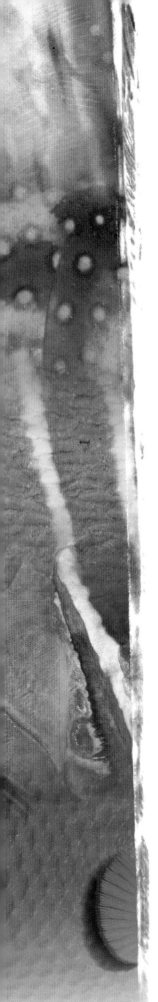

FURTHER INFORMATION

BOOKS

Arnold, Nick. *Swimming with Sharks*. *Wild Lives* (series). Scholastic (2004).

Byatt, Andrew, et al. *The Blue Planet: Seas of Life*. DK Adult (2002).

Cole, Melissa and Brandon Cole. *Coral Reefs: Wild Marine Habitats*. Blackbirch Press (2004).

Ganeri, Anita. *Animal Groupings*. *Nature Files* (series). Chelsea House (2004).

Hirschmann, Kris. *Moray Eel*. *Creatures of the Sea* (series). Kidhaven Press (2002).

MacQuitty, Miranda. *Shark*. *DK Eyewitness Books* (series). DK Children (2004).

McKay, George, et al. *The Encyclopedia of Animals: A Complete Visual Guide*. University of California Press (2004).

Morgan, Sally. *Fish*. *Animal Kingdom* (series). Raintree (2004).

Perrine, Doug. *Sharks & Rays of the World*. Voyageur Press (2003).

Spilsbury, Louise. *Classification: From Mammals to Fungi*. *Science Answers* (series). Heinemann Library (2004).

Townsend, John. *Incredible Fish*. *Incredible Creatures* (series). Raintree (2005).

Walker, Pam and Elaine Wood. *The Coral Reef: Life in the Sea*. Facts on File (2005).

Wallace, Holly. *Classification*. *Life Processes* (series). Heinemann Library (2001).

WEB SITES

www.coralreef.noaa.gov/outreach/thingsyoucando.html
Discover how to support the National Oceanic and Atmospheric Administration's (NOAA) Coral Reef Conservation Program.

www.cousteau.org
Visit the Cousteau Society's Web site to explore the Kids' Corner and other links.

www.enchantedlearning.com/subjects/sharks/index.html
Follow the links to learn more about various shark species.

www.fishcount.org
Participate in the annual fish count of the Reef Environmental Education Foundation.

www.nationalgeographic.com/earthpulse/reef/reef1_flash.html
Take a virtual dive on Australia's Great Barrier Reef.

www.sanctuaries.nos.noaa.gov/oms/oms.html
Explore the National Marine Sanctuaries protected by the United States government.

www.seaworld.org/infobooks/Sharks&Rays/home.html
Click on the red dots of the shark anatomy tour link for an interactive tour. Visit other links for more details, such as behavior, diet, and hydrodynamics of sharks and rays.

www.sharkresearch.com
Find out how researchers are working to study and protect these valuable species.

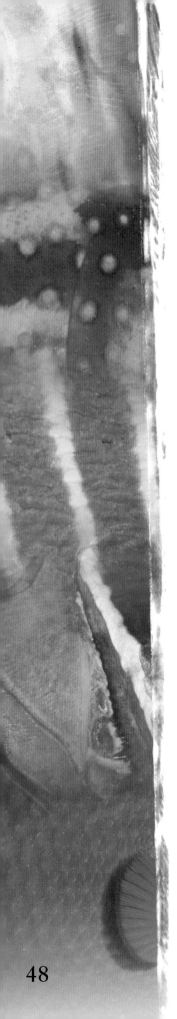

INDEX

Page numbers in **bold** refer to a photograph or illustration.